IN WILTSHIRE'S SKIES

IN WILTSHIRE'S SKIES

COLIN CRUDDAS

To Frank Edward Russell (1922–2004), my long-term friend and colleague during our days at Flight Refuelling Ltd.

Frontispiece: Perhaps only at Boscombe Down in the 1960s could a picture such as this be taken. Set against a background of rolling Wiltshire hills are examples of Britain's nuclear strike force. Clockwise from the top left are: Vickers Valiant, Avro Vulcan, Handley Page Victor, English Electric Canberra, HSA (Blackburn) Buccaneer and De Havilland Sea Vixen.

First published in 2004 by Tempus Publishing
Reprinted 2007

Reprinted in 2010 by
The History Press
The Mill, Brimscombe Port,
Stroud, Gloucestershire, GL5 2QG
www.thehistorypress.co.uk

Reprinted 2011, 2012

British Library Cataloguing in Publication Data.
A catalogue record for this book is available from the British Library.

ISBN 978 0 7524 3235 9

Typesetting and origination by Tempus Publishing.
Printed and bound in Great Britain.

Contents

Acknowledgements 6

Introduction 7

one Prelude 9

two Wings of War 25

three Peacetime Pursuits 42

four War comes to Wiltshire 57

five Testing Times 81

six Postscript 121

Bibliography 127

Acknowledgements

In writing a book of this nature, an author usually has to call upon a number of local experts he or she hopes will be prepared to donate their time and knowledge to his cause. My 'Wiltshire project' has certainly been no exception.

I therefore consider myself fortunate indeed to have co-opted the unstinted and generous assistance of so many willing colleagues. First and foremost I must thank Norman Parker, Tim Mason, Dave Berryman and Rod Priddle, who have contributed the vast majority of illustrations used in this book.

For lending their weight to my research efforts, the loan of much private material and the unfailing wisdom of their various comments, I also extend my deep appreciation to each of the following: Alan Jones's team at the Solent Sky Museum, John Pothecary, Dr Hugh Thomas, Peter Green, Mike Hooks, Mike Phipp, Barry Abraham, Frank Russell and *Aeroplane*'s editor, Mick Oakey.

My thanks also to the Defence Procurement Agency for allowing the use of many photographs still subject to Crown Copyright/MOD. These are reproduced with the permission of the Controller of Her Majesty's Stationery Office.

However, while every effort has been made to trace the source of copyright for other material used in this book, the author wishes to apologise for any inadvertent omissions or incorrect accreditation.

Finally, despite the ever-present demands of garden (large) and grandchildren (four, assorted), my wife, Thelma, has again brought her editing and proofreading skills to bear in producing the final result. For her patience and word processing effort, I am, as always, immensely grateful.

Introduction

Wiltshire is, of course, well known for the dawn ceremony held each Midsummer's Day at Stonehenge, but the county can claim a strong association with another dawn – that of military aviation in the British Isles.

The expansive downs of Salisbury Plain have proved an ideal setting for the many training and operational airfields constructed in and between the two world wars. Indeed, it may surprise many to find that the A303 arterial route to the south west, which today runs alongside the Stonehenge Heritage site, bisects an area that once housed a large Royal Flying Corps training establishment. Since it is military flying which has become predominately associated with the county and civil aviation that has prospered elsewhere in the county, the latter does not feature so prominently within these pages.

To compile a complete record of Wiltshire's historical links with the world of flying is well beyond the scope of this slender volume. Nevertheless, with a great deal of help from my friends, it has been possible to bring together this fascinating collection of images which well represents the county's strong ties with the 'third dimension'. Do enjoy!

Colin Cruddas
Shaftesbury 2004

The author caught in a reflective moment during National Service (1954–1956). This is the Drawing Office at the School of Land/Air Warfare, RAF Old Sarum (now a local Territorial Army HQ), where Corporal Technician Cruddas was draughtsman in charge of lecture aids production – a far cry from today's digital graphic presentations!

Wiltshire Bases

Location Definition	National Grid Ref.	Location Definition	National Grid Ref.
1. Kemble Airfield ★	ST 9696	21. Wanborough Relief Landing Ground	SU 2282
2. Blakehill Farm Airfield	SU 0791	22. Clyffe Pypard Relief Landing Ground	SU 0675
3. Long NewntonAirfield	ST 9292	23. Wroughton Airfield	SU 1478
4. Townsend Satellite Landing Ground	SU 0772	24. Yatesbury East Airfield	SU 0670
5. Hullavington Airfield	ST 9081	25. Yatesbury West Airfield	SU 0571
6. Lyneham Airfield	SU 0178	26. Ramsbury Airfield	SU 2670
7. Castle Combe Airfield	ST 8576	27. Marlborough Landing Ground	SU 1967
8. Colerne Airfield	ST 8071	28. Overton Heath Airfield	SU 1766
9. Melksham Landing Ground	SU 9061	29. Alton Barnes Airfield	SU 1062
10. Keevil Airfield	ST 9258	30. Upavon North Airfield	SU 1554
11. Conock Manor Landing Ground	SU 0656	31. Upavon South Airfield	SU 1555
12. New Zealand Farm Airfield	ST 9651	32. Everleigh Satellite Landing Ground	SU 2253
13. Tilshead Down Landing Ground	SU 0147	33. Netheravon Airfield	SU 1549
14. Rollestone Landing Ground	SU 1045	34. Bulford Fields Landing Ground	SU 1744
15. Shrewton Airfield	SU 0843	35. Larkhill Airfield	SU 1443
16. Stonehenge Airfield	SU 1141	36. Boscombe Down Airfield	SU 1740
17. Oatlands Hill Airfield	SU 0940	37. Porton Down Airfield	SU 2137
18. Lake Down Airfield	SU 1039	38. High Post Airfield	SU 1436
19. Zeals Airfield	ST 7733	39. Old Sarum Airfield	SU 1533
20. South Marston Shadow Factory Airfield	SU 1889		

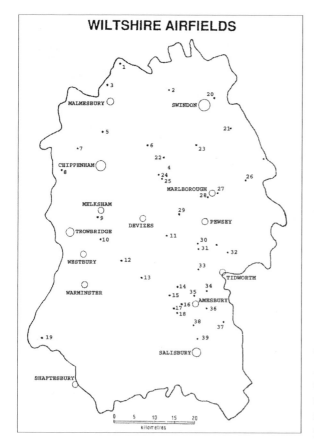

WILTSHIRE AIRFIELDS

★ Kemble is officially in Gloucestershire, although part of the airfield lies in Wiltshire. It has not, therefore, been included in this book.

The author is indebted to Barry Abraham and the Airfield Research Group for permission to reproduce this reference map and base data, first published in *Airfield Review* some years ago.

one

Prelude

Wiltshire's first modern-day recorded association with aviation was in 1909, when Horatio Barber erected a hangar at Larkhill near Durrington Down, a blustery open site in the middle of Salisbury Plain. From here he began to fly in a machine built to his own design at the Howard Wright factory in London's Battersea Park. Similar sheds were soon constructed alongside Barber's, to house an Henri Farman biplane belonging to G.B. Cockburn, and a Blériot monoplane owned by Captain J.D.B. Fulton. The following year, more hangar workshops were added, firstly for military use (although aeroplanes were not immediately available to fill them) and later for the Bristol Flying School: a venture set up to complement the Bristol company's successful activities at Brooklands and Filton. Official sanction for the building of the Bristol hangars at Larkhill had only been given on the understanding that visual sighting of the sun's rise on Midsummer's Day would not, in any way, be impeded. Accordingly, a 'sun gap' was provided between the buildings, which on more than one occasion proved its worth when an emergency called for a landing not over, but between the sheds.

The close proximity of the Bristol School to Wiltshire army camps soon encouraged an increased military interest in powered flight and led to the subsequent formation, in April 1911, of the Royal Engineers Air Battalion, No.1 Company operating lighter-than-air machines at Farnborough and No.2 Company 'conventional' aeroplanes at Larkhill. Then, in August 1912, the first official Military Aeroplane Trials took place at Larkhill, where Samuel Franklin Cody (actually Cowdery), flying his Cody V biplane (hastily cobbled together from two previously crashed machines), outpaced his rivals to win a total of £5,000 prize money. This was an enormous achievement for someone whose American prairie upbringing had barely included reading or writing but who had, nevertheless, managed to teach himself to fly!

The Bristol School of Flying ceased activities at Larkhill in June 1914 and combined with the company's Brooklands operation to form No.1 Reserve Squadron. The hangars they used still stand and serve as a poignant reminder of that far-off Edwardian era, even though the site has now been absorbed within the Military's School of Artillery. In recent times, in what is now Wood Road, a small plaque has been erected alongside the hangars, recording for posterity Larkhill's historic claim to fame.

Upavon, situated some five miles 'as the crow flies' from Larkhill, is now the oldest active airfield in Britain. Opened on 12 June 1912, it became the resident base for the RFC's Central Flying School – a role it retained, apart from a nine-year break (1926–35), for the next thirty years. It was while flying a Maurice Farman biplane from Larkhill to Upavon on 16 April 1913, that Lt Cholmondley of No.3 Squadron, aided by good luck, strong nerves and a full moon, demonstrated that night flying was supposedly within the capability of the average Service pilot. However, considering the difficulties frequently experienced by many pilots when coping with daylight flying during that early period, this claim may have been a little before its time.

In 1912, the Air Battalion of the Army took over unused cavalry school buildings near the village of Netheravon and the following year No.3 Squadron from Larkhill and No.4 Squadron from Farnborough arrived.

The importance of Larkhill had somewhat declined by mid-1914 and Netheravon now took on the somewhat dubious soubriquet of the 'Concentration Camp'. This followed the arrival of the Royal Flying Corps' Military Wing, which was brought in to evaluate the use of aircraft in what were then thought to represent wartime conditions. A large-scale project, it involved over 700 personnel, some 70 aircraft and a vast number of assorted support vehicles and equipment. Although, initially, tented accommodation had been the order of the day, a permanent station was established by 1914. Many of the original buildings featuring an unusual timbered panel construction are still in use today. Such then was aviation's growing influence on the county as the clouds of war gathered.

To complement Bristol's manufacturing activities at Filton, the company established flying schools at Brooklands and Larkhill (shown here) in 1910. Primary instruction was given on the Bristol Boxkite and more advanced work was undertaken on the Prier monoplane.

Captain Bertram Dickson was allocated a Bristol Boxkite for use in the army manoeuvres at Larkhill in 1910. He also contributed to the early success of the Bristol Flying School until failing health led to his premature death on 28 September 1913.

Above: Blériot pilot and engineer, Pierre Prier, was invited to join the Bristol design team at Filton in 1911. His single-seat monoplane, designed for the Gordon Bennett Cup Race, led to a family of two-seat machines in 1912. Prier is shown here with the Bristol-Prier P-1, No.46, at Larkhill in July 1911.

Opposite: Messrs Rainey and Fowler demonstrate the 'hold on tight and I'll show you what to do' method of flying instruction on the Bristol Boxkite.

Beyond the 'sun gap' are three pairs of hangars, built for military use by No.2 (Aeroplane) Company. This unit became No.3 Squadron when the Royal Flying Corps was formed in 1912 and is now the oldest unit in the United Kingdom to fly heavier-than-air machines. Bristol-Prier No.56 is in the foreground.

Harry Busteed (front cockpit) with pupil Eric Harrison, ready to depart from Larkhill in Bristol-Prier monoplane No.82.

Prier and Captain Dickson in the short fuselage Bristol–Prier No.73 at Larkhill. The ground assistant seems perilously placed should there be sudden forward movement.

Undercarriage supports and bracing are shown to good effect in this Bristol–Prier monoplane study.

After Prier left the company in 1912, Gordon England was persuaded by Sir George White to join his Bristol team as pilot and designer. This is the GE2, No.103, about to be flown by England in the Military Competitions at Larkhill in 1912.

The GE2, No.103, looking somewhat tired but pugnacious.

The suspended lower wing was an unusual design feature of the GE2.

Side-by-side dual control arrangements such as those on this GE2 were known as 'Sociable' designs. Flight instrumentation appears to be virtually nonexistent.

Military Trials were held at Larkhill in 1912 to determine the aircraft best suited for various roles. Thirty-one machines were entered but it was the Royal Aircraft Factory's B.E. 2 (Blériot Experimental) which, though undergoing the rigorous tests in a 'non-competitive' capacity only, put up the best all-round performance.

Despite the relatively impressive performance of the B.E. 2, it was the Cody V Biplane that was adjudged the overall winner of the Military Trials. After receiving £5,000 prize money and the Royal Aero Club's Gold Medal, Cody was surprised when a congratulatory message was received from the King, addressing him as 'Colonel'. Ever the showman, he needed little encouragement to continue using the honorary, if mistakenly conferred, rank.

A B.E. 2 piloted by Major Gerrard, Royal Marines, performs before Sir Horace Smith – Dorrien's entourage at a Military Review on Perham Down, 22 May 1913. This frequently used picture is said to record the first fly-past in history.

With the development of Upavon and Netheravon, Larkhill's military flying role decreased, and by late 1914, the old flying area was overrun by army camp buildings. The hangars built for Barber and Cockburn are visible in the centre of the skyline. Construction materials were transported using the railway track built as an extension to the Amesbury–Bulford line.

Perhaps looking a little forlorn, the Bristol Flying School's five hangars still stand and are, arguably, the oldest aeronautical buildings in the United Kingdom today.

Because aircraft and engines were unreliable and flying techniques still evolving, accidents were inevitable. On 5 July 1912, Captain E.B. Loraine and Staff Sergeant R.H.V. Wilson became the first RFC aviators to lose their lives on Salisbury Plain. Referred to as 'Airman's Cross', this monument recording the event is located at the junction of the roads leading from Amesbury to Shrewton (A344) and the A360.

The funeral procession of Captain Loraine, who died when his Nieuport monoplane crashed between Stonehenge and Shrewton, approaches Bulford railway station.

The Central Flying School opened at Upavon in August 1912 and soon eclipsed the training activities at Larkhill.

A Farman 'Shorthorn' prepares for take-off at Upavon.

It was not long before a surprising assortment of aircraft types became resident at Upavon. Here, Major E.L. Gerrard prepares for take-off in an Henri Farman. This picture from 1913 shows ground support being given by both army and navy personnel.

Prominent in this 1914 group of CFS instructors is the first commandant, Captain Godfrey Paine RN. Seated on his left is Major Hugh Trenchard, Royal Scots Fusiliers, who, as Sqdn Cmdr, effectively served as adjutant.

Central Flying School's B Flight at Upavon on a seemingly quiet day in mid-1914.

The large gathering of aircraft for 'wartime assessment' led to Netheravon being dubbed the 'Concentration Camp' in June 1914.

Typical of the aircraft involved in the month-long 'wartime assessment' was the B.E. 2a, which is shown here in the foreground, and the Maurice Farman S.11.

'Well, chaps, what do you think?' A Maurice Farman S.11 'Shorthorn' awaits a performance verdict at Netheravon.

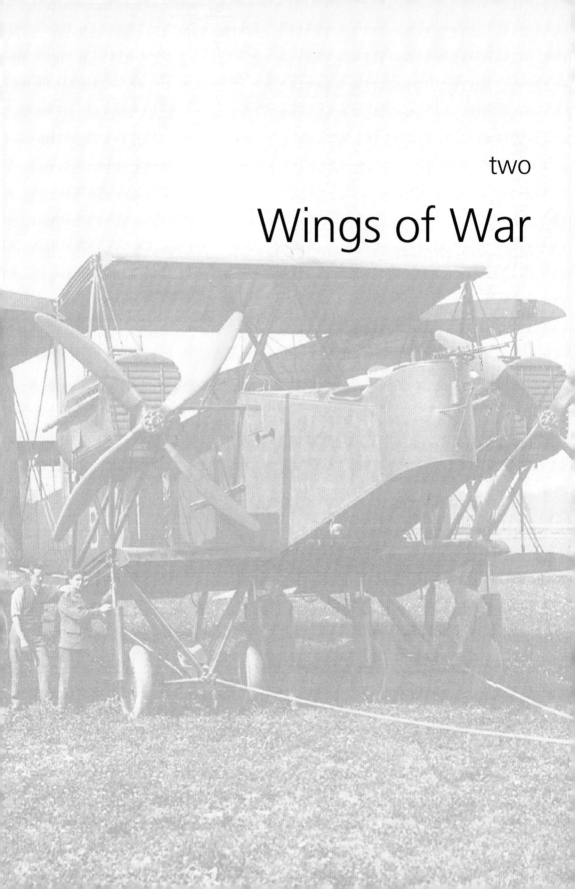

two

Wings of War

The outbreak of the First World War led to a vast increase in the mobilisation of manpower and resources. Nowhere was this more evident than in Wiltshire where large military encampments sprang up on Salisbury Plain. As the popular expectation of a short 'home-by-Christmas' war faded, more airfields began to appear in the county. In 1916, No.1 Balloon School was formed at Rollestone, near Shrewton, and No.36 and No.37 Training Depot Stations were opened at Yatesbury. The following year, specialist navigation and bombing schools were established at Stonehenge and other flying training bases created at Red House Farm (Boscombe Down), Ford Farm (Old Sarum) and Druids Lodge (Lake Down). A temporary airfield, situated between Tilshead and West Lavington, was also used by the RFC's No.105 Squadron. At most of these, in addition to Upavon and Netheravon, air and ground crew personnel of the American Expeditionary Force also received training in 1917/18.

Instrumental in the build-up of the airfields on Salisbury Plain was the Amesbury and Military Camp Light Railway. An extension of a main track first laid down in 1902, it was built as a military line to facilitate transportation of heavy materials to the new construction sites where, in many cases, German prisoners of war worked alongside 'colonial' and Chinese labourers under the supervision of the Royal Engineers.

By the end of the war, Wiltshire housed ten of the sixty-three training depot stations used by the RFC/RAF and by so doing, made a significant contribution to the country's wartime demands.

The construction of airfield sites required a transportation facility for the transfer of stores and material from central supply locations. The problem was overcome when Sir John Jackson built a railway system linking the new bases on Salisbury Plain to the railhead at Amesbury.

In the period immediately before and after the outbreak of war in August 1914, Netheravon served as a training centre. Later, it was more involved with the build-up of new squadrons for the air war in France. This typical training course photograph is dated 10 July 1914.

Mishaps were expected and happened frequently at the early training establishments. This B.E. 2c, however, was turned over by a strong wind while taxiing across the airfield at Netheravon.

The occasional loss of an aeroplane due to gusty weather conditions was of little consequence compared to the calamitous damage caused at Netheravon during the great storm of 29 October 1918.

Size does not always protect. This Handley Page O/400 also paid the price after it was caught out in the open on 29 October 1918.

Above: Upavon consisted of twin aerodromes (north and south) either side of the road, linking Andover to Upavon. As with all the major airfields on Salisbury Plain, it was mainly concerned with training pilots during the First World War.

Right: Whatever happened to the likely lads? Some trainee aircrew were issued with flying kit at the School of Gunnery, Uxbridge, before arrival in Wiltshire.

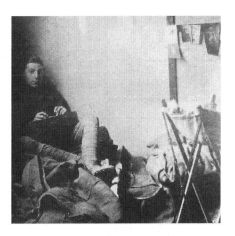

Considering Yatesbury's training role, it is unlikely that Lieutenants Rider and Griffen are striking a victory pose.

A quiet moment during training at Yatesbury.

Above: Seen here at Yatesbury, the Royal Aircraft Factory's R.E.8, or 'Harry Tate', as it was more commonly referred to, entered service with the RFC in 1916. The ungainly 130hp RAF engine installation with twin vertical exhaust pipes provided a ready recognition feature.

Opposite top: BE.8, *424* at Upavon CFS in August 1915. Though the two–place version was used for training, this type had to be operated as a single-seater when used in the bombing role.

Opposite middle: A Sopwith Camel at a Wiltshire training depot. The airman striking a nonchalant pose on the far wing-tip appears to be American. This highly manoeuvrable machine was the most successful fighter used by the British in the First World War.

Opposite bottom: These two Airco D.H.1s belonging to No.59 Reserve Squadron were among the assorted training machines used when the twin airfields at Yatesbury East and West opened in 1916.

A mixed bag at Yatesbury in July 1917. Accompanying Sopwith Pup, *A6193*, (left) are two Avro 504 Ks.

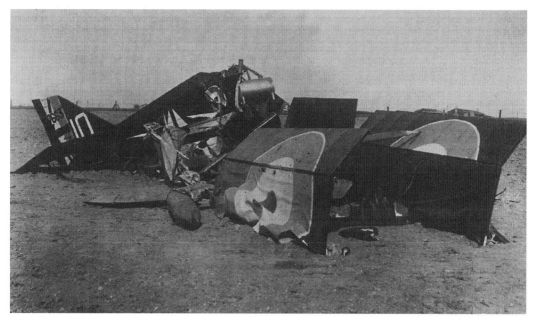

This D.H.6, in which Captain Vinsen came to grief at Yatesbury, failed to grace the skies again.

'Home of the heavies'. Stonehenge aerodrome, opened in 1917, was used by the School of Navigation and Bombing.

The road destined to become today's A303 (top left of picture), leading to the West Country, bisects the area occupied by the Stonehenge aerodrome in 1918.

Aircraft ground movement, 1918 style. A Handley Page O/400 is persuaded to 'move along' by a Clayton tractor. Formed as part of No.14 Training Depot Station at Stonehenge, the so-called Handley Page Flying School, relocated from Marston in Kent to Stonehenge in January 1918, was used to provide instruction on heavy bomber types. It was not, as the name might imply, operated by the Handley Page company.

Handley Page O/400, *C9685*, runs up its Rolls Royce Eagle VIII engines at Stonehenge.

This D.H.9, *H4273*, based at Stonehenge, crashed at what is now known as Woodhenge, after 'beating up' a football match. Although the two occupants were unhurt, a soldier walking to the match was killed. The event occurred in late 1918.

Although their names are not recorded, members of No.207 Squadron appear happy enough pictured alongside a H.P. O/400 at Stonehenge.

The small café on the right-hand side of the Amesbury–Shrewton road was a popular rendezvous for passing motorists in the mid-1920s. It was demolished, along with the pair of cottages on the left, in 1936–37. Stonehenge aerodrome (top left) was closed in 1920.

No.6 Training Depot Station was established in October 1917 at what was originally Red House Farm, but soon became officially known as Boscombe Down. At first, it consisted of tented accommodation and six BE tents – so-called because they were 'T' shaped to house a B.E. 2. This bird's-eye view from 24 February 1918 shows that it was not long before more permanent facilities were also in place.

By the end of the First World War, Old Sarum had been in operation for just over a year as No.11 Training Depot Station. Today, the site remains essentially unchanged from its appearance here on 28 September 1918.

The classic 80ft-span Belfast roof trusses, for what are now listed buildings at Old Sarum, were erected with the assistance of German prisoners of war. Six aeroplane sheds, an aircraft repair shed and two motor transport sheds were constructed, along with other accommodation for specialised trades. The 1918 Motor Transport section is shown here.

The station ambulance at RAF Old Sarum, 1918.

A Bristol F.2b. Fighter with the Iron Age Castle Rings fortification below. Old Sarum aerodrome can be seen right of centre, and the 'Beehive' cottage bus stop, familiar to thousands of servicemen returning to camp, is just discernible at the centre of the road junction.

A Bristol F.2b. Fighter taxies in across Old Sarum's lush grasslands.

Lake Down became 14 Training Depot Station in 1917, boasting an impressive array of technical and administrative accommodation.

Above: These German prisoners of war may be a long way from home, but they do not seem entirely displeased with life at Lake Down in 1918.

Left: Even further away from home is this member of the United States Air Service, undergoing training at Lake Down.

Opposite above: Victory celebrations at Lake Down in November 1918. The Union Jack, Stars and Stripes and the Tricolour share pride of place.

Opposite below: Today, all that remains of Lake Down aerodrome is the water tower. Now alongside the A360, it once stood in the centre of this bustling camp.

three

Peacetime
Pursuits

When peace was declared in late 1918, the manufacture of war machinery in Britain came to a grinding halt. It also brought about the closure of many Service establishments. Within a year the number of operational stations used by the Royal Air Force fell from over 300 to 45, with Stonehenge, Lake Down and Yatesbury among those feeling the cold wind of closure. Netheravon, however, became the administrative centre for the disbandment of many operational units and its Flying Training School continued to provide instruction for RAF and Royal Navy pilots.

Larkhill, now relocated to Knighton Down, assisted Old Sarum in the training of Army Co-operation squadrons while, at Upavon, the Central Flying School's activities continued in full swing throughout the 1920s.

Somewhat surprisingly, the Balloon School at Rollestone was also retained and, in 1920, was renamed the School of Balloon Training. It maintained this function until 1939 when the RAF's Anti-Gas School took over the camp.

Most of the many training machines that seemed to be in constant flight around Salisbury Cathedral's spire in the mid-1930s were Hectors, Audaxes, Lysanders, Blenheims and Ansons. Of unique interest, however, were the Cierva C.30 autogyros which, first seen when Sir Alan Cobham's touring air display visited several Wiltshire towns in 1932, were later used in military trials at Old Sarum.

Alongside military flying, civil light aircraft operated from private landing grounds at Frome, Melksham, Tisbury, Marlborough and Trowbridge. Of special note is the airfield used at Conock Manor by Colonel R.R Smith-Barry, inventor of the dual-approach to aircrew training in the First World War.

At High Post aerodrome, situated midway between Salisbury and Amesbury, the Wiltshire Light Aeroplane and Country Club was formed in 1931. Its tenure was relatively short, however, because, like all private flying ventures, it was forced to close when war broke out in 1939.

Although deemed surplus to requirements in the early 1920s, Yatesbury was reprieved in 1936. No.2 Camp (West) reopened as No.10 Elementary and Reserve Training School administered by the Bristol Aeroplane Company, and in 1938 the Royal Air Force's No.2 Electrical and Wireless School also took up residence at No.1 Camp (East).

As unease regarding Germany's warlike preparations increased, the Royal Air Force Expansion Scheme, initiated in 1934, began to gather momentum during the late 1930s and new permanent stations appeared around the country. In Wiltshire, these included Hullavington, Colerne, Lyneham and Wroughton, although not all of these had become fully operational when war finally erupted in 1939.

The reader may at this stage wonder at the seeming omission of Boscombe Down. However, such is the long-running and unique contribution made by this famous establishment that a later chapter, 'Testing Times', has been entirely devoted to its development.

Opposite above: Despite the post-war closure of many Service aerodromes, Netheravon continued to host No.1 Flying Training School and even expanded in 1924 to provide training for Fleet Air Arm pilots. Fl. Lt Woodhouse and Sgt Sheppard fortunately escaped with only slight injuries when their training flight in D.H.9A, *E902*, came to this abrupt end on 1 December 1923.

Opposite below: In 1924, the Central Flying School was joined at the Upavon South airfield by No.3 Squadron, equipped with Sopwith Snipes.

Bristol Bulldog IIAs of No.17 Squadron which, with No.3 Squadron, flew from Upavon South in the mid–1920s.

By 1935, the CFS had been re-equipped with the Avro Tutor.

The Hawker Hart shared the CFS' advanced training role with the Avro Tutor in the mid-1930s.

A crisp portrayal of the CFS establishment at Upavon in the late 1930s. Immediately facing the concrete apron are Avro Tutors with Hawker Audaxes behind. Exercising its modern, twin-engined monoplane superiority is a lone Airspeed Oxford.

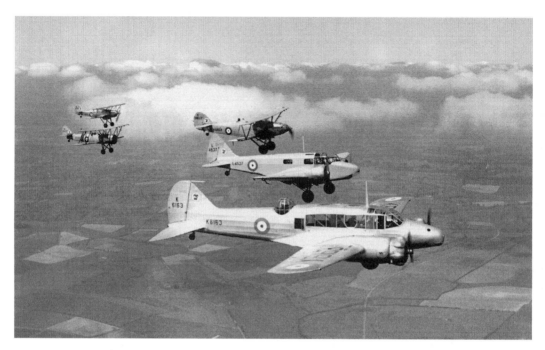

This fine air–to–air study shows the variety of aircraft at CFS's disposal in 1938. From (top) left to right: Hawker Fury, Avro Tutor, Hawker Audax, Airspeed Oxford and Avro Anson.

The CFS Avro Tutor aerobatic display team gets in a spot of practice, c.1938.

Yatesbury (West) was reopened in 1936 as a Reserve Training School administered by the Bristol Aeroplane Co. The School's fleet of Tiger Moths is shown here lined up in faultless order.

This Yatesbury airmen's hut, ready for inspection, is a sight to either gladden or terrify many an ex-serviceman. This form of 'bull' certainly extended over the post-war National Service years, as the author can verify!

Old Sarum became the main home for Army Co-operation squadrons in Wiltshire during the pre-war period. Here, an Armstrong Whitworth Atlas *J9531*, of No.16 Squadron, flies over its base in 1924.

The clear outline of the site of Salisbury's first cathedral and the adjacent Castle Rings again provide the almost obligatory background for this Old Sarum-based Avro 504N, *J9260*, in 1929.

The airfield at Old Sarum, shown here after the war, had changed little from that originally laid out in 1917. Although no personnel appear to be in attendance, the Gloster Grebes seem busy enough.

The Hawker Hector first entered service with the RAF in 1937. It subsequently equipped No.16 and No.59 Squadrons at Old Sarum. This photograph was for No.59 Squadron's Christmas card of 1938.

The distinctive cowling lines of the Hector's 805hp Napier Dagger twenty-four cylinder engine are evident in this aerial study of *K9700*. The pilot is Wg Cdr G.H.D. Evans.

This Hector, *K9690*, displays the standard camouflage paint scheme adopted by RAF squadron aircraft following the Munich Crisis of 1938.

During the Empire Air Display at Old Sarum on 29 May 1937, this No.16 Squadron Hawker Audax, *K3698*, stalled in a 'Prince of Wales Feather' manoeuvre. It crashed on the airfield in full view of the spectators, killing Pilot Officer Ronald Elms.

This fine study shows an Avro 681 Rota I, *K4232*, on the approach to Old Sarum. Early Service trials of the autogyro in the mid-1930s were not entirely successful, but RAF interest was resurrected during the Second World War when several machines were used for radar calibration work.

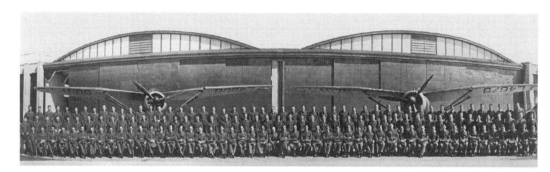

A typical squadron photograph showing No.16 Squadron at Old Sarum. Both the Lysanders saw service in the Middle East. *L4679* suffered a landing mishap on 3 June 1942 and *L4686* was shot down by an Italian Fiat CR.42 on 16 October 1940.

Westland Lysanders replaced No.16 Squadron's Hawker Audaxes in 1938. The oversized squadron codes and two-colour (blue/red) roundels were a distinctive feature of Service markings in the late 1930s.

Continuing the county's training theme, a flight of Audaxes depart from Hullavington in 1938. Although production of this type ceased in 1937, it remained in RAF service well into the war.

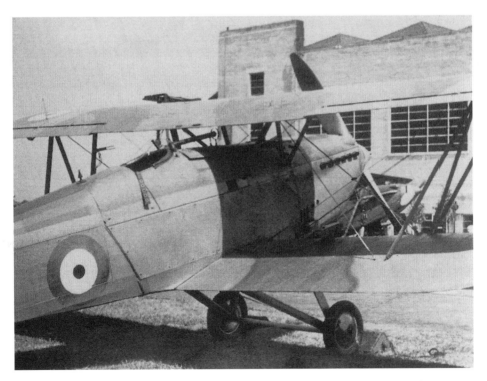

By 1939, the biplane fighter had been largely superseded by more modern monoplane designs. Here, two Hawker Furies of No.9 FTS await their fate at Hullavington in July 1939.

Closing this inter-war chapter on a civil note is this picture of the airfield used by the Wiltshire School of Flying (hangar and clubhouse top right). It shows the High Post Hotel and airfield on the far side of the Salisbury–Amesbury road (A 345) in the mid-1930s. Salisbury is off to the left.

four

War comes
to Wiltshire

Although the pre-war Royal Air Force Expansion Scheme had, with foresight, created numerous new airfields, once the war began the construction of many more soon got under way. However, the need for more operational bases was matched by the requirement to increase aircraft production. This challenge was met, in part, by accelerating completion of 'shadow factories', such as that at South Marston near Swindon. This allowed the Phillips and Powis Aircraft Company to start production of the largest order for training aircraft ever placed by the government. (A total of 3,450 Miles Masters were eventually manufactured by this firm at its Woodley, near Reading, South Marston and Doncaster sites). To reduce the threat of possible German attention to such an imminently large target, it was decided to relocate parts of the South Marston complex to sites at nearby Blunsdon and Sevenhampton. This enabled assembly work to be carried out, not only on the Master trainer, but also on the Short Stirling bomber, after attacks on the Short factories at Belfast and Rochester necessitated relocation to a separate site (FS2) on the north-east corner of South Marston's airfield in 1941.

When manufacture of the Master ceased in 1943, Vickers Supermarine laid claim to the main site where they then concentrated on the Griffon-powered Spitfire Mk 21. As the war progressed, conversion and modification work was also carried out on many varied Service types, both British and American.

Prior to its occupancy of South Marston, Supermarine had, following devastating raids on its Southampton works, diversified Spitfire assembly and flight testing throughout the neighbouring counties of Wiltshire, Hampshire and Berkshire. This proved to be a highly complex operation which, along with the massive Spitfire assembly facility at Castle Bromwich, near Birmingham, called for exceptional management skills. Foremost among the Wiltshire locations were Salisbury and Trowbridge with High Post (and Chattis Hill in Hampshire) and Keevil their respective flight-test airfields, though many smaller concerns were also involved.

Although the Wiltshire bases were associated with many offensive operations during the conflict, as in the First World War, their efforts were mainly concentrated on training. RAF Colerne, for example, though housing several night-fighter squadrons, also accommodated a succession of maintenance and flying training units. Later, in 1945, it became home to the Gloster Meteor, the only Allied jet fighter to see operational service in the Second World War.

Salisbury Plain's training role received royal recognition when King Gorge VI witnessed 'Exercise Exeter' – a spectacular precursor to the D-Day airborne landings – at Netheravon. Glider activity continued at Netheravon until 1945, when it began to focus more on aircraft and equipment trials. Upavon provided flight training, No.7 Flying Instructors School being equipped with Airspeed Oxfords. The popular Oxford, the Avro Anson, Percival Proctor and de Havilland Tiger Moth commanded the skies over Yatesbury as a demand grew for aircrew possessing specialised radio and wireless-operating skills.

At the outbreak of war, the School of Army Co-operation at Old Sarum was operating a mixed bag of Lysanders, Blenheims, Ansons and Hectors. A variety of other, unusual, light aircraft were also delivered for trials, which eventually led to the formation of Auster-equipped Air Observation Post squadrons. These were to prove highly successful in the North African and European land campaigns from 1942 onwards. No.41 Operational Training Unit, which was created at Old Sarum in September 1941, also contributed to the development of Army co-operation and air support when their vulnerable Lysanders were replaced by Curtiss Tomahawks, and later Mustangs, in the tactical recce role.

Alongside the many aerial activities, there was, in 1944, another task of quite a different nature underway at Old Sarum, and that was the waterproofing of hundreds of RAF vehicles prior to the sea-borne landings in Normandy on D-Day.

The preparation and despatch of aircraft and equipment to the front line squadrons fell to Maintenance Units such as No.76 and No.15 MU based at Wroughton. It was there, for example, that many Airspeed Horsa gliders were finally assembled and test flown, towed by Whitley, and later Albemarle tugs. Several thousand aircraft were received at Wroughton for modification work between 1941 and 1945 – a truly magnificent contribution to the Wiltshire war effort. No less deserving of praise were the Herculean tasks undertaken by No.33 MU and the various units within Ferry Command at Lyneham. Ferry Command was formed in July 1941, when it took over from the Atlantic Ferry Organisation (ATFERO). Lyneham was then set up as the receiving base for many aircraft flown directly from the USA, and the training centre for long-range flying and navigation. In 1943, Lyneham also became a major UK terminal for British Overseas Airways Corporation, and during the same year, Ferry Command was transformed into No.45 Group within the new Transport Command.

During the extreme winter of 1939/40, Hullavington, then still under construction, was the scene of severe hardship. Airmen living in tented accommodation were frequently exposed to flooding and freezing conditions before domestic improvements were finally put in place, at which point, in 1942, the Empire Central Flying School took up residence. In addition, the station served as a major aircraft storage area and, at its peak, had over 1,000 aircraft on site awaiting disposal instructions. Closely associated with Hullavington, Castle Combe was a relief landing ground before achieving full training-station status, but water logging and constructional difficulties constantly compromised its serviceability.

Zeals was another Wiltshire airfield badly affected by prolonged adverse weather conditions, despite which it remained an active operational fighter station until its transfer to the Fleet Air Arm in 1945.

Blakehill Farm and Ramsbury were two important RAF and USAAF bases, both with major roles in transport, communications and airborne forces operations. It was from these stations that many gliders were towed and parachute troop divisions carried by Dakota transports to support the D-Day, Arnhem and Rhine crossing operations. Once bases were established in France, the Dakotas were utilised to ferry the many casualties back to their Wiltshire stations in what are now termed 'casevac' missions.

Numerous other locations in Wiltshire provided crucial wartime service and support. Within this category are Clyffe Pypard, Alton Barnes, Wanborough, Manningford, New Zealand Farm and Long Newnton, all of which were sites providing elementary flying instruction. Also deserving of mention are the satellite airfields and relief landing grounds created at Oatlands Hill, Tilshead Down, Shrewton, Townsend, Overton Heath, Bulford Fields and Rollestone, and the bombing/gunnery ranges at Beversbrook, Chiseldon, Hillmartin and Pepperbox Hill.

Above: Work began on the 'shadow factory' and airfield at South Marston in 1940. This Miles Master III, *W8513*, was one of 1,100 such training machines built by Phillips and Powis Aircraft Ltd at South Marston.

Right: The Short Stirling was the first four-engined bomber to enter service with the RAF. Designed to meet Air Staff Specification B12/36, the first prototype took to the air on 14 May 1939. Following the Luftwaffe's raid on Rochester in August 1940, production was allocated to areas which included a new assembly plant at South Marston. Here, Air Transport Auxiliary ferry pilot, Joan Hughes, is about to deliver a Stirling to a Service squadron.

Following heavy attacks on the Supermarine works at Southampton, Spitfire production and flight testing were dispersed to locations in Wiltshire and elsewhere. One such site was the Fore Street Garage in Trowbridge. Here, accompanying Queen Mary during a royal morale-boosting visit, are, from left to right: Vernon Hall (Vickers Supermarine area manager), James Bird (director and general manager) and Len Gooch (works manager).

This purpose-built factory at Bradley Road, Trowbridge, was used for Spitfire component manufacture.

Keevil aerodrome, which opened on 15 July 1942, served as a base for USAAF and RAF airborne operations and, after D-Day, resupply missions for the Special Operations Executive (SOE). In addition, Vickers Supermarine test pilots undertook the flight testing of Spitfires assembled on the airfield. Here are two Spitfire Mk XVIIIs at Keevil.

Wessex Motors Ltd in New Street, Salisbury, was one of several premises requisitioned in Wiltshire for Spitfire production.

After basic fuselage construction was completed at the Wessex Motors site, units were moved to the Wilts and Dorset bus garage, in Castle Street, for the attachment of tailplanes, engines and systems components.

Vickers Supermarine carried out final assembly and flight testing of Salisbury-produced Spitfires at High Post airfield and at Chattis Hill (just over the county boundary in Hampshire). This evocative picture shows an Mk 22, *PK312*, (nearest) and two Mk 21s, *LA215* and *LA232*, which, though built at Castle Bromwich, were all flight tested at High Post.

A tragic event occurred on 13 September 1944, when the hybrid prototype Supermarine Spiteful, *NN660*, (a Spitfire Mk XIV with new laminar flow wing) crashed near High Post. Following a low-level mock 'dog-fight' with another Vickers test pilot, the aircraft hit the ground, killing the pilot, Frank Furlong.

A cold start for this Defiant night fighter and a scene typical of that at Colerne during the harsh winter of 1940/41.

Later declared unsuitable for offensive operations, the Defiant was relegated to target-towing duties. The four-gun turret was replaced with a simpler canopy for the target winch operator.

A spectacular prize claimed by Colerne's night fighters was a Heinkel HE 177, shot down by a Mosquito NF XIII of No.151 Squadron on 21 January 1944. This picture shows an HE 177 of the victim's parent unit, KG 40, which, after capture by the French Resistance, was transferred to the UK – rather surprisingly acquiring 'invasion stripes'.

In January 1945, Colerne became the first station to accommodate, on a permanent basis, the jet-powered Gloster Meteors of No.616 (County of Yorkshire) Squadron. No.74 Squadron's Meteor Mk IIIs are shown after arriving a little later in May 1945.

This photograph shows an airborne unit about to depart on a training demonstration in October 1941. The press is much in evidence! Although the location is the No. 1 Parachute Training School at Ringway near Manchester, this scene typifies the work undertaken at Netheravon and other Wiltshire bases. On display are Whitley troop carriers, a Westland Lysander, two G.A. Hotspur gliders and a Hawker Audax.

Royal visitors attended 'Exercise Exeter' at Netheravon on 19 May 1944.

'Pay attention – I shall only tell you once!' Student glider pilots receive instruction on the Hotspur training glider.

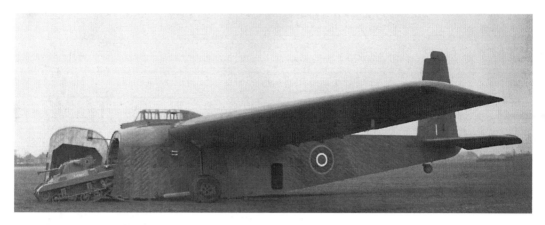

The Hamilcar heavy glider, used in 'Exercise Exeter', discharges a T-19 Locust tank.
Alternatively, this glider could convey two Bren gun carriers, a self-propelled Bofors gun or two
armoured scout cars.

The sheer size of the all–wood Hamilcar is shown here to good effect. Following a combat
landing, a tank would simply be driven straight through the unopened nose!

A Halifax disgorges stores containers during 'Exercise Exeter'. Parachutes of different colours allowed easy identification of various stores.

This classic picture captures the essential training role of Upavon. A Master III (top), Oxford and Magister of the Central Flying School in 1942.

Although the date of this picture and the Tiger Moth's unit are not recorded, the landmark is one that became familiar with thousands of trainee aircrew in both world wars.

'Away from base', this CFS flight of Tiger Moth, Magister and Oxford is backed up by a more belligerent Whitley bomber.

A D.H. 89 Dominie, *HG691*, (foreground) and Percival Proctor of No.2 Radio School,
Yatesbury.

A trainee wireless operator is put through his paces in the Dominie.

In addition to its use as a trainer, the Percival Proctor IV was highly regarded as an ideal light communications aircraft.

This tired-looking Avro Anson, *N5331*, is typical of many used for general aircrew training at stations throughout the country during the wartime years.

The Auster AOP III equipped nine specialist Air Observation Post squadrons following successful trials at Old Sarum.

Forever associated with its wartime Army Co-operation role, this Auster I, *LB312*, flies over Old Sarum in more recent times. It is piloted here by its long-time owner, John Pothecary.

Left: Presenting a warlike appearance are these Curtiss Tomahawks, a type used by No.41 OTU at Old Sarum.

Below: This striking photograph shows Armstrong Whitworth Albemarles used for glider testing by 15 MU at Wroughton.

Aircraft types of all shapes and sizes were received at Wroughton's Maintenance Units for modification and onward despatch to units at home and overseas. Here is a Fleet Air Arm Grumman Tarpon (Avenger).

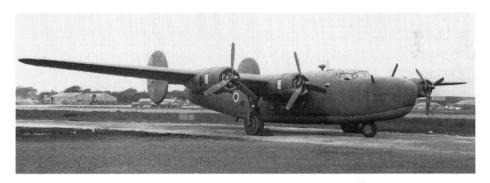

It is perhaps the Liberator and Avro York transports that best symbolise the types that operated from wartime Lyneham. This Liberator C. Mk VII is pictured in July 1944.

Lyneham is the UK arrival venue for this assortment of military personnel. Judging by the shorts worn by one officer, this Avro York has travelled from, at least, the Middle East.

The mail must get through, and helping it on its way are these WAAFs loading a 511 Squadron Liberator in seemingly chilly conditions at Lyneham.

Two Spitfire MkIIs and a Hurricane MkIIA of the Empire Central Flying School flying near Devizes. The ECFS was formed at Hullavington in March 1942, in order to pool experience gained in the RAF's worldwide flying training organisation.

Although there is no positive proof that this picture was taken at Hullavington, it clearly demonstrates the cosmopolitan nature of an ECFS course. The accompanying aircraft are a Short Stirling, B-25 Mitchell and Douglas Boston.

No.9 Service Flying Training School at Hullavington operated the Rolls Royce Kestrel XXX-powered Miles Master Mk I trainer during the early part of the war.

Zeals served as a forward-operating airfield within No.10 Group Fighter Command from May 1942. In early 1945, however, the Glider Pick-up Training Flight arrived with Dakotas and CG-4A Hadrian gliders. The unit's task was to train pilots in the American 'snatch' technique of recovering gliders from previously used landing zones.

The elongated hook below the Dakota has caught the glider's towrope suspended from two poles placed several feet apart. This technique was first used by the Americans in Burma and further developed by the Airborne Forces Tactical Development Unit at Netheravon.

Opposite: Hullavington's aircraft storage role is well illustrated here. Although not easy to identify, Stirlings and Mosquitos appear to dominate the scene.

When RAF Zeals transferred to the Fleet Air Arm, it became known as HMS Hummingbird. However, the Navy's tenure was short and after only a few months, on 1 January 1946, it was decommissioned – but not soon enough to save this Corsair!

6 June 1944: D-Day. Dakota transports and glider tugs towing Horsa gliders departed from Blakehill Farm for France. Over the ensuing weeks Nos 233 and 271 Squadrons proceeded to fly supply-reinforcement and casualty-evacuation missions to and from Blakehill Farm.

> WHEN YOU PAUSE TO SEE THE TIME OF THE DAY REMEMBER THE CANADIANS
> WHO FLEW FROM THIS AIRFIELD BRAVE AND COURAGEOUS, SOME NEVER
> RETURNED, OTHERS RETURNED WITH LIFETIME MEMORIES.
>
> DEDICATED BY THE MEMBERS OF 437 (T) HUSKY SQUADRON WITH THE
> GRACIOUS HELP OF THE PEOPLE OF CRICKLADE ON 25TH SEPTEMBER 1994
> NO. 437 SQUADRON ROYAL CANADIAN AIRFORCE R.A.F BLAKEHILL FARM
> 14TH SEPT 1944 - 7TH MAY 1945

No.233 Squadron and No.437 Squadron of the Royal Canadian Air Force participated in the Arnhem airborne operation. Blakehill Farm's Dakotas also formed part of the massive fleet of seventeen squadrons that towed British gliders across the Rhine. This plaque, commemorating the Canadian effort, was unveiled in 1994.

five

Testing
Times

M any official establishments have served British aviation with distinction over the past century, but none more so than Boscombe Down. Its present-day reputation for excellence as a testing centre is universally regarded as second to none.

The airfield opened on 1 October 1917 and soon afterwards became No.6 Training Depot Station, one of several located in the Salisbury Plain area. In addition to providing training for many Royal Flying Corps and, from 1 April 1918, Royal Air Force pilots, over 300 American air and ground crew personnel also received instruction there when their country entered the war.

As a result of peacetime cut-backs, Boscombe Down was closed on 1 April 1920 and the general area returned to pasture, but a renewal of official interest led to the site reopening in September 1930.

The first bomber units to arrive were Nos 9 and 10 Squadrons, equipped with Vickers Virginias, to be joined in February 1931 by the Porton Down Experimental Flight. This consisted of four aircraft used solely to assist the neighbouring Chemical Defence Experimental Station (CDES). It was not until 1937 that the resident operational squadrons' lumbering biplanes (by now, Handley Page Heyfords) were replaced with modern counterparts, such as the Whitley, Anson and Battle.

At the outbreak of war, Boscombe Down was the first airfield to use Standard Beam Approach Equipment – a major technical advancement that used radio beams to assist pilots during a landing approach. At the same time, and because of its close proximity to the Larkhill experimental bombing range, the station developed a close association with airborne armament and bombing techniques. These activities coincided with the arrival, in early September 1939, of the Aeroplane and Armament Experimental Establishment (A & AEE), which was relocated from Martlesham Heath in Suffolk, as it was considered vulnerable to enemy attack.

With the simultaneous departure from the airfield of No.88 and No.218 Squadrons' Fairey Battles to France, the station was transferred from Bomber Command's administration to that of Flying Training Command. However, the transition from an operational to a largely testing role put a considerable strain on the administrative system. In order to fulfil the A & AEE's already proud legend 'Probe Probare' (Properly to Test), new facilities were urgently required to cope with the rapid influx of new machines and associated equipment. High on the wanted list was a dedicated bombing range. Accordingly, Ashley Walk, an area of some 5,000 acres in the New Forest, was chosen, and eventually came into operation in July 1940. Despite bureaucratic difficulties and the appalling weather conditions during the first winter of the war, Boscombe Down settled into its new and important role. It did not, however, totally relinquish its operational status and continued to house, on a temporary basis, various fighter units. One of these, No.249 Squadron, became involved in a memorable incident while carrying out patrol duties during the Battle of Britain. On 16 August 1940, two days after arrival, one of its pilots, Flt Lt James Nicholson, engaged a Messerschmitt 110 over Southampton. In spite of his Hurricane sustaining considerable damage, and he, himself, being severely injured, he managed to maintain sufficient control to shoot down the enemy aircraft before baling out. His eventful mission, almost brought to an end by a shotgun blast from a local Home Guard sergeant, earned Flt Lt Nicholson the Victoria Cross for his bravery.

Throughout the wartime period, specialist tasking units at Boscombe Down, such as the High Altitude Flight and the Intensive Development Unit, put more than 1,400 British and American aircraft and an impressive array of Allied equipment through the Service-approval process. This eventually led to the construction of a 3,000-yard runway to accommodate four-engined machines such as the Stirling, Lancaster and Halifax.

Once established as A & AEE's permanent home, testing responsibilities were divided into separate categories. New and modified aircraft along with weapons were evaluated by A Squadron (fighters), B Squadron (bomber, transport and large civil aircraft) and C Squadron (naval aircraft).

During the later stages of the war, a number of captured German aircraft were also received for comparative evaluation. Created in 1950, D Squadron evolved from the Airborne Forces Experimental Establishment based at Beaulieu in Hampshire, which concentrated on the testing of helicopters and specialised airborne equipment. Also after the war, the Civil Aircraft Test Section undertook the vital function of airworthiness certification of large civil aircraft, before this, in turn, was taken over in 1950 by the Air Registration Board. In the early 1960s, E Squadron joined the testing sections to look into the suitability for Service use of new transport and communications aircraft. Working in tandem with these operational evaluation units were the RAF's Handling Squadron, which produced aircrew documentation, and the renowned Empire Test Pilots School (EPTS). The latter, founded at Boscombe Down in 1943, moved elsewhere in 1945 but returned in 1968 to become an integral part of what was now the country's premier testing establishment.

Since 1991, the administration of Boscombe Down has undergone many far-reaching changes. All the research flying previously carried out at Farnborough and Bedford was transferred to Wiltshire in 1994, and the newly formed Defence Evaluation Research Agency (DERA) then assumed responsibility for conducting research programmes side-by-side with the evaluation of aircraft and airborne equipment for all three Services. This resulted in a combined resident test fleet of some forty aircraft.

In July 2001, DERA split into two separate organisations, the Defence Science and Technology Laboratory (DSTL) which, as part of the Ministry of Defence, continues to handle sensitive areas of research, and QinetiQ plc. As a public private partnership, QinetiQ competes in the field of innovative solutions to customer problems within the scientific/industrial sphere. This includes the area of Service-approved testing once undertaken by the now defunct A & AEE.

This brief history has outlined the varied and important roles undertaken by Boscombe Down. Though still faced with the challenge of changing requirements, it is today on course to continue spearheading UK aerospace testing for the foreseeable future.

Opposite top: This Fairey Fox, *J9025*, was one of the first aircraft to form the Porton Experimental Flight. Originally based at Netheravon, the unit was transferred to Boscombe Down in February 1931.

Opposite middle: As the 1930s progressed, the number and variety of test aircraft assisting Porton Down increased. Taken on the unit's strength was this Armstrong Whitworth Whitley, *K4587*.

Opposite bottom: A Wellington Mk I, *L4228*, was also modified to carry smoke and chemical discharge equipment.

Right: Contained in the Whitley's bomb bay was a Smoke Curtain Installation (SCI). This was an official euphemism for a chemical agent dispersal unit.

Below: Porton Flight technicians install a large SCI into the bomb bay of Wellington, *L4228*, in May 1940.

Even after the direct threat of invasion had passed and the need to provide retaliatory chemical weapons had receded, work continued to develop equipment and delivery techniques. A typical underwing SCI installation is shown here.

Lysander, *T1501*, is sporting an undercarriage sponson-mounted SCI.

Fairey Albacore, *L7142*, was used for underwing SCI trials in late 1941.

Following the departure of No.88 and No.218 Squadrons' Fairey Battles to France in September 1939, Boscombe Down became the new home for the A & AEE.

Left: It was while flying Hawker Hurricane Mk II, *P3576*, from Boscombe Down that Flt Lt James Nicholson of No.249 Squadron won Fighter Command's only Victoria Cross. He died while serving with south-east Asia Command in 1945 when his Liberator crashed attacking Rangoon.

IN MEMORY OF
JAMES NICOLSON VC
1917 – 1945
On the 16th of August 1940 Flight Lieutenant James B. Nicolson was leading Red Section of No. 249 Squadron from RAF Boscombe Down. An attack by enemy aircraft whilst over Southampton left Nicolson wounded and his Hurricane on fire. When about to bail out he sighted and shot down one of the attacking aircraft, only then did he abandon his own aircraft. For this deed of gallantry Nicolson was awarded the Victoria Cross, the only member of Fighter Command to be so honoured during the war.

During the 1940–45 period, over 1,400 aircraft were subjected to specialised Service and investigative testing at Boscombe Down. The following pictures are a representative selection.

A & AEE's arrival at Boscombe Down brought with it a fleet of aircraft that had already been under test at Martlesham Heath, including this Handley Page Hereford I, *L6002*.

The second prototype Westland Whirlwind, *L6845*, shows its modified horn-balanced rudder and interim engine exhausts. Although possessing many unique design features, the Whirlwind was only a qualified success as a fighter–bomber, equipping just two RAF squadrons, No.263 and No.137.

A wolf in sheep's clothing! Guaranteed to challenge the local spotting fraternity was this Messerschmitt Bf 109, *AE479*. This aircraft had force-landed in France in November 1939 and, after delivery to A & AEE, was evaluated in mock combat against contemporary British fighters.

F. Hills & Sons Ltd produced this unusual Bi-Mono experimental aircraft in 1941. It was intended to take off as a biplane and, after jettisoning the top wing, continue as a monoplane.

Opposite top: F. Hills & Sons Ltd were allocated Hawker Hurricane Mk I, *L1884*, for further jettisonable wing development. This 'one-off' hybrid was known as the Hillson F.H. 40 Slip-Wing Hurricane. However, the wing was never jettisoned in flight and the trials were soon terminated.

Opposite middle: A Harvard II and the Hillson Slip-Wing Hurricane are at a Boscombe dispersal, *c.*1942.

Opposite below: The Westland P. 12, *K6127*, powered by a Bristol Mercury XII engine, was designed as a four-gun tail turret 'beach strafer', but by the time this strange looking machine first flew on 27 July 1941, the requirement had passed. Nevertheless, trials were conducted at A & AEE to prove the concept.

Providing an interesting comparison are these two views of the prototype Fairey Barracuda, *P1767*.

First flight tested with a fuselage-mounted tailplane, this aircraft was later flown featuring it braced and attached high on the fin, as subsequently fitted to production aircraft.

F.G. Miles' innovative approach to design produced the Miles M. 20, which he considered would be cheaper to manufacture than the Spitfire or Hurricane. Designed to Ministry Specification F. 19/40, this machine, one of only two prototypes, displayed a fighter performance equal to that of the Hurricane, despite the drag-inducing fixed undercarriage. The success of the Hurricane in the Battle of Britain prevented further development of the Miles project.

Looking decidedly businesslike in October 1941 is the second prototype Lancaster I, *DG595*. Note the 'bulged' bomb doors, ventral turret and early style exhaust flame dampers.

We are talking serious Lancasters here! This classic official photograph shows a very pristine Lancaster Mk II, *DS602*, powered by four Bristol Hercules VI engines at Boscombe Down in October 1942.

The underside of this Lancaster I, *L7528*, warrants inspection. Note the pivoted hook for airfield- (not deck!) arrested landings, the ventral turret and what appears to be a specially modified bomb door fairing, 16 November 1942.

This trials report photograph from 27 July 1942 shows an Avro Lancaster I, *R5609*, disporting well-braced Air to Surface Vessel (ASV) radar aerials. Seventy-three different Lancasters were tested at A & AEE during the wartime period.

Let us not forget who was first in the four-engined bomber queue! Short Stirling Mk III, *R9309*, stands firmly to attention at B Squadron's dispersal in June 1942.

A little further down the testing line came this Handley Page Halifax III, *HX226*. Following a complete redesign of the fin and rudder and the fitment of Bristol Hercules XVI engines (shown here), the Halifax proved a worthy companion to the Lancaster.

Avro Anson IV prototype, *R9816*, was fitted with Wright Whirlwind R-760-E1 engines and variable pitch airscrews. This was a trial installation evaluated at Boscombe Down prior to the shipment to Canada of 223 specially built airframes (minus engines).

Undergoing trials in mid-1942, the first prototype Avro York, *LV626*, featured a twin fin and rudder arrangement. All production Yorks had a third central fin fitted to improve lateral control.

This Douglas Boston III, *BZ201*, assumes a 'menacing pose' at Boscombe Down. In the background a Blackburn Botha and Vickers Wellington appear less threatening.

Also undergoing tests at A & AEE is this ex-No.88 Squadron Douglas Boston III, *W8315*. Note the trial installation dorsal gun turret and the clearly discernable gap between fin and rudder.

This rather stark photograph shows Spitfire Mk III, *N3297*. It featured a Rolls Royce Merlin XX engine with two-speed supercharger and clipped wings for improved rate of roll. Only two Mk IIIs were built.

One of the many American types supplied to Britain under the Lend-Lease Agreement was the Lockheed Ventura patrol bomber. Shown here is a Ventura II, *AE939*, awaiting A & AEE's attention in January 1943.

A well-worn Ventura and its equally well-worn crew at Boscombe Down. Many newly trained pilots experienced difficulty coping with the excessive torque on take-off generated by the Ventura's Pratt and Whitney Double Wasp engines.

The first of three prototype Blackburn Firebrand F. Mk Is, *DD804*, arrived at A & AEE for a month's performance testing in late June 1942. Originally conceived as a naval fighter, continual changes in operational requirements deferred the Bristol Centaurus-powered Mk IV torpedo strike variant's entry into service until 1945.

Over 3,000 Kittyhawks were delivered to Commonwealth Air Forces under the Lend-Lease arrangement. Here, Curtiss Kittyhawk IIA, *AL229*, is about to embark on testing at Boscombe in April 1942.

One of the more unusual types in Wiltshire's wartime skies was the Vultee Vengeance dive-bomber. This example is Vengeance IV-2, *FD243*. Following America's entry into the war, a large number of these machines, already being produced for the RAF, were diverted to the USAAF. Most of those that eventually arrived in the UK were converted to target-tugs.

Shown here at Boscombe Down is Consolidated Liberator IX, *JT578*. The large single fin was a distinguishing feature of the civil variant *AL504* 'Commando', often used to transport Sir Winston Churchill and other dignitaries to overseas destinations.

Still bearing its US serial number *4133*, this North American Mustang Mk IV became *TK589*, one of two Mk IVs dedicated to trials work at Boscombe Down.

More American hardware – this time a Northrop P-61 Black Widow night fighter. Although fully evaluated at Boscombe Down in 1944, this impressive twin-boom aircraft did not see service with the RAF. It was, however, used extensively by the USAAF and USN in both the European and Pacific war theatres.

Illustrating the armament development carried out at Boscombe Down throughout the war (and up to the present day), is this Spitfire Mk IX, *MH477*, equipped with American M 10 Tube Cluster Rocket Launchers, in March 1945.

Keeping good company with a Northrop Black Widow is de Havilland Mosquito B XVI, *ML994*, resident at A & AEE for armament trials in October 1944.

Let it not be forgotten that the Fairey Swordfish remained in Service use throughout the war! Pictured here is the 4 x 60lb rocket installation on *DK747*, in 1943.

Not to be outdone in the biplane department was this Vickers Supermarine Sea Otter, *JM739*. Comparative tests with its predecessor, the Walrus, were inconclusive, although the Sea Otter did possess longer range and could carry a heavier payload.

This A & AEE Squadron flight of 1946 symbolises the arrival of the jet age. Leading the Spitfire Mk 24 and Vampire Mk I is a Meteor Mk III.

The prototype Reid and Sigrist Desford first flew on 9 July 1945. It then underwent airworthiness certification trials with the Civil Aircraft Test Section at Boscombe Down.

Built in the Experimental Hangar at Hursley Park, near Winchester, the Vickers Supermarine E.10/44 prototype, *TS409*, was first flown from Boscombe Down on 27 July 1946 by Jeffrey Quill.

Sqdn Ldr T.S. 'Wimpey' Wade is flying the Hawker 1052 prototype, *VX272*, from Boscombe Down in 1948.

The first prototype Fairey Gannet, *VR546*, then known as the G.R.17, shortly after its arrival at A & AEE in September 1949. The later introduction of a third cockpit required auxiliary fins to be added to the tailplane.

Fitted with a 2,000hp Rolls Royce Griffon 56 piston engine, the Blackburn Y.A.8, *WB788*, first flew on 3 May 1950. This was one of two aerodynamic test vehicles evaluated at A & AEE prior to the delivery of the Double Mamba–powered Y.B.1. Competitive trials with the Y.B.1, Short S.B.3 and the Fairey G.R.17 eventually led to the latter (i.e. Gannet) winning production contracts.

The world's first pure jet transport was this Vickers Viking, *VX856* (later *G-AJPH*). This Rolls Royce Nene-powered machine gained its civil certificate of airworthiness at Boscombe Down, where this picture was taken on 6 February 1950. Note the unusual 'twin wheels in parallel' undercarriage arrangement.

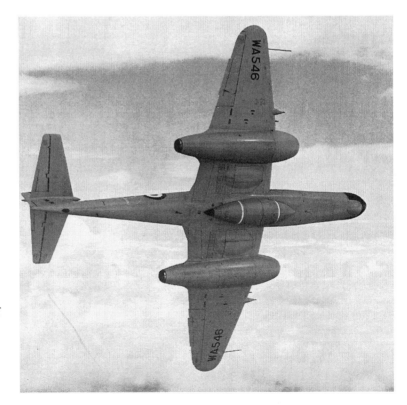

A pleasing study of the first prototype Meteor NF.11, *WA546*, during A & AEE trials, *c*.1950.

Meteor NF.11, *WM367*, undertook the last flight of this variant from Boscombe Down on 23 August 1972.

Many other Meteor marques were tested at A & AEE. This F.8, *WA982*, is seen in A & AEE's care on 17 March 1952.

Manufactured at Fairey's Heaton Chapel Works at Stockport, the sole F.D.1, *VX350*, was transported by road to Boscombe Down. Flown for the first time by Fairey's chief test pilot, Gordon Slade, on 12 March 1951, this aircraft provided useful aerodynamic and handling data for the company's record-breaking F.D.2.

In January 1952, this Convair B-36, *492042*, fell short of the runway at Boscombe Down after a non-stop flight from Forth Worth, Texas. Within several days, the aircraft, which had incurred only superficial damage, was repaired and flown back to the US.

This is Supermarine Swift F.3, *WK220*, undergoing 'work in progress' at A & AEE in late 1954. It is to be hoped that the sizeable nose ballast box was clearly marked 'Remove before flight'!

Frequently gracing the skies over Boscombe Down and (as often witnessed by the author) at Old Sarum, were Hawker Sea Hawk F.B.3s engaged in mock ground-attack exercises. This picture, taken on 7 October 1954, shows *WF284* equipped with Red Angel rocket projectiles.

This interesting mix of Venom, Meteor and Dragonfly helicopter is dwarfed in Boscombe Down's Weighbridge Hangar by the Blackburn B.101 Universal Freighter 2, *WZ889*. When later brought up to Beverley standard, this machine was registered as *G-AMVW*. The picture is dated 1 April 1954.

The Handley Page Hastings was no stranger to Boscombe Down. It was tested in many guises, including this engine test-bed configuration. Replacing the two outboard Bristol Hercules engines on *TE583* are the Armstrong Siddeley Sapphire turbojets intended for the Victor bomber.

Tailplane finlets were fitted on the Westland Wyvern S Mk 4 to offset rudder–lock under certain flight conditions. This picture of *VZ774* was taken at Boscombe Down on 30 August 1954.

Bristol Sycamore *WT993*, is shown 'somewhere in the West Country' flying from Boscombe Down on 15 November 1954.

A Scottish Aviation Twin Pioneer C.C.1, *XL968* against a perfect rural Wiltshire background on 24 July 1956.

Saunders Roe produced two SR.53 rocket-assisted jet interceptor prototypes in the mid-1950s. Here, *XD145* test runs its de Havilland Spectre rocket motor. *XD151* was destroyed in a fatal accident at Boscombe Down on 15 June 1958.

Above: The Fairey F.D.2, *WG774*, piloted by Peter Twiss, achieved the absolute world airspeed record of 1,132mph while based at Boscombe Down on 10 March 1956.

Left: Miss Lettice Curtis who, after serving as a 1st Officer with the Air Transport Auxiliary between 1940 and 1945, spent the early post-war years as a technician and flight test observer at the A & AEE. Later she joined the Fairey Aviation Co. as a senior flight development engineer and was closely associated with the Gannet test programme at Boscombe Down.

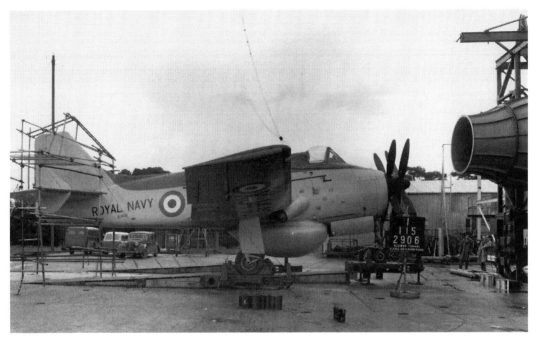

The prototype Fairey Gannet A.E.W.3, *XJ440*, prepares for testing in Boscombe Down's Blower Tunnel on 22 December 1958.

Once heard, never forgotten! Both the Mamba-powered Gannet and Sapphire-engined Javelin (in background) had very, *very* distinctive sound signatures.

Presumably not intended to frighten the enemy, this Westland Whirlwind H.A.R.2, *XJ759*, is shown bedecked as a 'Disney Special' in December 1958.

Boscombe Down's Vickers Valiant B(PR)K.1, *WZ376*, engages with Gloster Javelin F.(A.W.) 9, *XH865*, during air–refuelling trials.

An H.P. Victor B.1 undergoes refuelling compatability trials with a USAAF tanker at Boscombe Down in the early 1960s.

Boeing KB-50J refuelling tanker, *9383*, at Boscombe Down during Operation 'Floodtide' on 20 February 1961.

Representing the RAF's transition to second-generation jet fighters is this A Squadron grouping. The Folland Gnat (centre) and Percival Jet Provost (top right) trainers first appeared on the Squadron in 1959.

The sights and sounds at Boscombe Down in the mid-1960s would have included this Bristol 192 Belvedere H.C.1, *XG449*, with A & AEE's Rotary Wing Test Squadron.

A de Havilland Sea Vixen, Boulton Paul Balliol, Fairey Gannet and HSA (Blackburn) Buccaneer of C Squadron in 1966.

A & AEE's Canberra B.2, *WV787* and Avro Vulcan B.1, *XH478*. This particular Canberra, equipped with a special bomb-bay tank and retractable spray boom, took part in chemical agent dispersion tests. Later, it was used as the water spray tanker for testing Concorde's anti-icing systems.

This picture shows TSR 2, *XR219*, rolling to a graceful halt in September 1973, just prior to its cancellation.

Lockheed Hercules W.2, *XV208*, 'Captain Beaky', served with A & AEE's Meteorological Research Flight in the 1990s.

six
Postscript

Although, today, little tangible evidence remains of Wiltshire's mighty wartime effort, it is appropriate to mention activities now taking place at some of the remaining sites.

High Post no longer reverberates to the sound of aero engines. The former flying club and Spitfire assembly hangar are now more quietly occupied by light industry; Netheravon has become the Army Air Corps helicopter base, the HQ of the Brigade of Gurkhas, and the Joint Services Parachute Centre; Hullavington, now renamed Buckley Barracks, houses No.9 Supply Region's Royal Logistic Corps – at the same time, it is available to Nos 621 and 625 Volunteer Gliding School Squadrons for a limited amount of flying; Colerne has also reverted to army use and is now known as Azimghur Barracks, and Bristol University's No.3 Air Experience Unit uses its gliding facilities; Upavon, now Trenchard Lines, is the headquarters of the Adjutant General's Department, the Provost Marshal's Office and the Army Training and Recruiting Agency, and No.622 Volunteer Gliding School and the Army Gliding Association use the airfield for their activities.

Today, little has changed at Keevil since wartime days. Lyneham's Hercules use it for tactical training, and at weekends the skies, once filled with Horsa and Hadrian gliders, now play host to the gentler pursuits of the Bath and Wiltshire Gliding Club; Lyneham is the RAF's Hercules transport base. Nos 24, 30, 47 and LXX Squadrons are currently resident. It is forecast, however, that the transport and tanking duties performed by the Hercules will soon be transferred to Brize Norton. Wroughton has for many years housed the Science Museum's not inconsiderable reserve aeronautical collection; South Marston, once such a thriving element within the British aircraft manufacturing industry, is now the main European production plant for the Honda motor company. Although an expanding business park now exists at Old Sarum, it is a real pleasure to record that there is also still a virile flying club on site and that its unique atmosphere and historic grass airfield continue to serve as a fine present-day tribute to all that has gone before.

This Cessna C.34 Airmaster, *G-AFBY*, was at High Post when civil flying resumed in 1946. Due to its close proximity to Boscombe Down, the airfield closed in 1947.

Today, Netheravon's modern-style control tower bears little resemblance to the 'square block' design of wartime years.

Hullavington-based No.1 Air Navigation School operated several twin-engined types of trainer, including this Vickers Wellington T.10, *RP353*, until the school's closure in mid-1954.

A present-day reminder of Hullavington's RAF connection is this turf-covered L-type hangar.

From one Hercules to another. Flight Refuelling Ltd's Mk 17B Hose Drum Unit provides a drink for a thirsty receiver during an air-refuelling practice mission.

Post-war South Marston. Aircraft production continued until January 1961, when the last
Vickers–Armstrongs Supermarine Scimitar was built. Component manufacture for other products
within the Vickers Group went on until the site was purchased by the Honda Motor Co. in 1981.
Here, the flying control area and detuner/silencing pen at South Marston is shown. With Swift
FR. 5s much in evidence, the date of this picture is probably late 1950s.

A group of notable Vickers Supermarine test pilots. From left to right: Les Colquhoun, Mike Lithgow, Jeffrey Quill, Guy Morgan and John Derry.

When you've got to go! The formal port of entry for countless servicemen over the years. Old Sarum's guardroom, by then considered structurally unsound, was demolished in 2003.

And what could be a more pleasant note on which to close – a beautiful sunny day with the Flying Club in full swing at Old Sarum. Old Sarum's Air Observation Post squadrons are commemorated on this plinth-mounted plaque.

Selected Bibliography

Britain's Military Airfields (1989), David J. Smith, ISBN 1-85260-038-1
Action Stations 5: Military Airfields of the South-West (1982), Chris Ashworth, ISBN 0-85059-510-X
Wiltshire Airfields in the Second World War (2003), David Berryman, ISBN 1 85306 703 2
Wings Over Wiltshire (2003), Rod Priddle, ISBN 1-901-587-34-7
Spitfire – The History, Eric B Morgan and Edward Shacklady, ISBN 0-946219-10-9

If you are interested in purchasing other books published by The History Press,
or in case you have difficulty finding any of our books in your local bookshop,
you can also place orders directly through our website
www.thehistorypress.co.uk